THE 5-POINT LAND BUYING CHECKLIST

Proven Ways to Help Make Buying Land Easy

by Bryan Lark

Integrity, excellence, and simplicity in the land business

TABLE OF CONTENTS

ENDORSEMENTS	5
INTRODUCTION	14
YOU'VE JUST GOT TO KNOW YOUR...	17
ACCESS (20 POINTS)	31
LOCATION (20 POINTS)	37
LAYOUT (20 POINTS)	46
DEVELOPMENT POTENTIAL (20 POINTS)	50
PRICE (20 POINTS)	62
DUE DILIGENCE	66
WE'RE HERE TO HELP	70
SPECIAL BONUS OFFER: 10% OFF	73

THE 5-POINT LAND BUYING CHECKLIST

PROVEN WAYS TO HELP MAKE BUYING LAND EASY

BRYAN LARK

Copyright © 2023 by Bryan Lark

All rights reserved. No part of this publication may be reproduced, distributed, or transmitted in any form or by any means, including photocopying, recording, or other electronic or mechanical methods, without the prior written permission of the publisher, except in the case of brief quotations embodied in critical reviews and certain other noncommercial uses permitted by copyright law.

THE 5-POINT
LAND BUYING
CHECKLIST

ENDORSEMENTS

You know, as a long-time land investor, I've come across loads of guides and books, but I've got to say, Bryan Lark's e-book, "The 5-Point Land Buying Checklist" stands out in the crowd.

What's it about? Well, it's like a trusted friend guiding you step-by-step through the land buying process. It's a fantastic resource - something I wish I had when I started out. Bryan's deep understanding and love for the land business really come through. This e-book breaks down the complex world of land buying into an easy-to-follow checklist. It's like a roadmap, keeping you on the right path, helping you avoid the usual potholes, and showing you how to maximize your profits.

Whether you're just starting out, or you've been buying land for a while, you'll find this book invaluable. Bryan's tips and insights are like a secret weapon for anyone looking to make their mark in the land market. Trust me, you don't want to miss this!

Mark Podolsky AKA The Land Geek, Owner of *Frontier Equity Properties* & *GeekPay.io*.

As a seasoned Land Investor, I am thrilled to endorse Bryan Lark's e-book, "The 5-Point Land Buying Checklist." This comprehensive guide is an invaluable resource for anyone considering buying land. Lark's expertise shines through as he lays out a practical and systematic approach to buying land. The points based checklist offers a step-by-step framework that ensures you make informed decisions, mitigate risks, and maximize returns. Whether you're a novice or an experienced land buyer, this book is a must-read. Lark's insights, combined with his passion for land, make this e-book an essential tool in your journey to success in the land market.

Erik Peterson

Owner, *Landopia.com*, Land Investor, and *Land Geek* Coach

Bryan Lark is a true land expert. He has the know-how, experience, and process to make finding your perfect property easy and fast. He has distilled his wealth of land-buying wisdom into a simple and quick read that anyone can understand.

If you're in search of land, trust Bryan Lark to be your guide. His book will help you navigate the process effortlessly and find the property of your dreams.

Tate Litchfield
Everland Equity, Land Investor,
Land Geek Coach

Bryan Lark is undeniably a master in his field, an expert in the complex terrain of land acquisition. His knowledge is vast, his experience is extensive, and he has developed a process that simplifies your search for the ideal property.

Lark has synthesized a wealth of wisdom on land acquisition into a comprehensive yet accessible text. If you're on the journey to secure land, I strongly recommend Bryan Lark as your guiding hand. His book elucidates the procedure, allowing you to seamlessly identify and secure your dream property.

Jaren Barnes

Lead Educator at the *Land Maverick Society*

Bryan Lark knows land. He has the experience, process, and knowledge to make the search for your perfect property simple and fast. He has captured his land-buying wisdom and packaged it all in an easy to understand and quick read.

Jeremy D Brown
CEO of *Legacy Acres and Throne Publishing Group*, author of 13 books

Purchasing land can be overwhelming. Bryan will patiently and knowledgeably take you through the process of securing the perfect property for you and/or your loved ones. And, as you get to know Bryan through the process, you will experience his servant heart and sincere desire to put you above the idea of 'business.'

This same mentality is communicated through his e-book. Take the time to read the e-book and ask questions. You will grow confident that you are in good hands.

Dave and Jess Parmerlee
LTR Land

"When it comes to buying land, I can't think of anyone better than Bryan Lark to turn to for practical advice. He has the knowledge, experience, and integrity that you can trust for all your land buying pursuits.

In his typically generous spirit, he has written a very useful guide to help you not only understand the process of buying land, but also having the confidence to take action."

Larry Murrell
Owner/Member of *Mustang Land, LLC*

THE 5-POINT LAND BUYING CHECKLIST

INTRODUCTION

Hi! My name is Bryan Lark, and I'm the grateful owner of ZeteoLand.com – a Christian owned and operated land business whose mission is to provide you with the highest level of integrity, excellence, and simplicity in your land buying and selling experience. You can learn more about me and my business by visiting zeteoland.com/aboutus.

When it comes to buying land, there are a ton of items to consider. For the first-time land buyer, the purchase process can be quite overwhelming and even scary. Not only can you make a big mistake in buying a **bad** property, but you can also make a big mistake in **not** buying a **great** property.

Maybe you've heard horror stories about someone buying a "dud" of a piece of land and having difficulty with the property for years with no end. Maybe you've had a family member that bought a piece of land only to have it become the worst purchase of their lives. Or maybe you've heard some other type of bad land purchase and you just want to make sure that you don't make the same mistakes.

Well, you've started at the right place in reading this e-book. I'm happy to share my experience and knowledge with you to help you be a more informed land buyer and to experience land ownership as a blessing and not a curse. Make sure to read to the end of this e-book for a very special gift just for you!

THE 5-POINT
LAND BUYING
CHECKLIST

YOU'VE JUST GOT TO KNOW YOUR...

So... how do you find a great property? An even better question may be, "*How can I own a great property at a great price?*" Well, fear not! I want to share with you my **5-Point Land Buying Checklist** to help you become an educated land buyer that avoids some of the big pitfalls others have fallen into.

For you to be a successful land buyer, it is 100% necessary that you determine what your **purpose** is for buying land. **You've just got to know your purpose!** If you're thinking, "*I just want to own some dirt*", then you're not off to a very good start. Without knowing your purpose for buying, you're going to be like a sailboat in the Atlantic Ocean without a sail. You'll eventually get somewhere, but it may not be where you really want to go.

So, what are some good purposes for buying land? Here are my top 6 purposes (and not necessarily in priority order):

1. You're wanting a safe long-term investment.

Over the centuries, land has consistently been about the safest investment there is and has averaged anywhere from 5-10% appreciation annually. One of the wealthiest men in history said it best when he said, *"The major fortunes of the world have been made in land"* (John D. Rockefeller). If you're wanting a relatively safe place to put your money, consider what many call *"land banking."* The idea here is that you've got some cash, but you really aren't interested in the low interest rate that your local bank is offering with their savings account or CD. For the average person, I'd say that this purpose is perhaps the highest and best purpose for buying land. Land will always have value and if the past is any indication of what's to come, it will continue to appreciate over time. Buying a piece of land today at $10,000 will prove to be worth far more than that in 5-10 years from now. And as an added bonus, you don't have to do much to keep it. It just sits there, and no one can steal it from you.

2. You're looking for a quick "flip."

A word of caution here: Flipping land can be a great idea for some but certainly not for the average person. There is a ton of due diligence and information you must know before you can make a profit. Just because you think it's a good deal will never guarantee that you can sell it for more than you bought it for. Never, ever buy real estate with the purpose of "flipping" unless you have a deep understanding of your market, which means understanding comps, market trends, sell-ability of the land, holding costs, improvement costs, and other related items. Imagine trying to flip a piece of land and waking up to the reality that you bought the land at much too high a price to even think about selling it for a profit. And now, you're stuck with it. Not a good place to be!

3. You're looking for a place to build a home.

If you're thinking about building that home you've always dreamed of, you can't build it in the air. It's got to sit on a piece of land. So, by necessity, you're going to need to buy a piece of land. This is a great purpose for buying a piece of land, but you'll want to make sure you buy the right piece of land that will allow you to build the home you want to build. You'll want to know about the local building codes, zoning codes, county restrictions, and utilities that are available.

Know your costs before building. Perhaps Jesus said it best when he said, *"Suppose one of you wants to build a tower. Won't you first sit down and estimate the cost to see if you have enough money to complete it? For if you lay the foundation and are not able to finish it, everyone who sees it will ridicule you, saying, 'This person began to build and wasn't able to finish'"* (Luke 14:28-30).

4. You're looking for a recreational property.

Like to hunt? Want a place to camp? Enjoy rockhounding? Looking for a place to just get away and listen to the birds sing? Would your family enjoy a place to have a monthly picnic at? What about a place to ride ATV's, dirt bikes, or four-wheelers? All these reasons could be great but as previously mentioned, you really want to ensure **before** you buy the land that you can actually do what you want to do on it. For example, you go out and buy a piece of land because you thought it would be excellent for hunting.

You saw deer on the property for years and you knew it was just going to be a great "honey hole." But imagine after buying it that you find out that you can't hunt because the land is just inside the city limits. Yep - those big bucks are just going to laugh at you and taunt you for the rest of your life. There will probably even be a record sized buck that sticks his tongue out at you!

5. The land presents you with an opportunity that meets a direct interest you have.

This is a much narrower purpose for buying land and you **really** need to make sure that the opportunity you think is available is actually available. The best example I can think of would be mining. Let's say that you're getting into mining, and you want a place to dig and find that big gold nugget you've always dreamed of finding. You hear about a piece of land out in the middle of nowhere that's for sale. You call up the owner and he tells you that there's gold on it everywhere.

The land is terribly ugly and you know it's more than you should pay but because of what you've heard, you get "gold fever" and decide to buy it before anyone else finds out about it. Well, all I can say is that you had better hope there's gold on the property - and not just gold 3,000 feet below the surface! In the famous words of a great US President, *"Trust but verify."*

6. You want to leave a family legacy.

Careful with this one! Just because you think it would be a "blessing" to your kids and grandkids when you're gone doesn't make it so. A piece of land you intended to be a blessing could end up as a curse. Over the years, there have been thousands and thousands of pieces of land that were passed down as a legacy only to become a "bur" in the saddle of every family member that followed. Imagine this scenario: A loving patriarch of the family decides to buy a 500-acre ranch to leave as a legacy to his children, grandchildren, and great grandchildren. He passes away and the land goes to his four children. Then years later, two of the children pass away leaving their portion to their children (the grandchildren). Then one of the children and three of the grandchildren want to build their home on the land. Well, who decides which part of the land they can build on? That turns into a fight and some of the family wants to sell the land, but the others don't. That brings up another family fight and a decision is never reached but unfortunately, the family no longer speak to each other because of all the drama that was caused. The land just sits there, and no one even goes there to enjoy it for fear that one of the other family members might be out there at the same time. What was meant to be a legacy has now become a curse. So, be careful! If this is your purpose, make sure to have a very detailed arrangement of what will happen to the land and how it will be managed and apportioned to each descendent after you're gone.

Alright, do you have your purpose now? Great!

Let's get right to our **5-Point Land Buying Checklist**. Whether you're buying a $1,000 piece of land or a $10,000,000 piece of land, the items in this checklist are crucial for you to understand and can save you a lot of stress, time, energy, and money.

As we move forward, you'll want a way to measure a property and compare its "score" to other potential properties you may buy. For each of these 5 points, you'll want to assign a value or score of 20 points. In theory, this would mean that a perfect property (which there aren't any) would receive a score of 100 points. Make sense?

You could even put together an evaluation scale something like this:
- Great buy = 85-100 points
- Good buy = 70-84 points
- A score of less than 70 is to be avoided or considered speculative.

As you score a potential piece of land, remember that your scores are most likely going to be fairly subjective. You get to score the property based on your own observations and preferences but just make sure that you score each property yourself so there is consistency in your evaluations.

5-POINT LAND BUYING CHECKLIST SCORING

ACCESS:	20 Points
LOCATION:	20 Points
LAYOUT:	20 Points
DEVELOPMENT POTENTIAL:	20 Points
PRICE:	20 Points
TOTAL:	?

OVERALL LAND SCORING

85-100 Points	=	GREAT BUY!
70-84 Points	=	POSSIBLE GOOD BUY
50-69 Points	=	AVOID THIS
0-49 Points	=	RUN!

THE 5-POINT LAND BUYING CHECKLIST

THE 5-POINT LAND BUYING CHECKLIST

ACCESS
(20 Points)

Though these 5 points are not necessarily in any specific order, I intentionally put this one in first. Here's why: If you can't access the property, then you really have no property unless of course, you fly in by helicopter each time you want to visit.

So, what do I mean by "access"? There are different types of access. Here are a few to consider:

Legal:

The first and most important type of access is legal access. Simply put, can you legally access your property? Some properties may be "landlocked" and in order to access them, you may have to cross over someone else's property to get to yours. And if there is no easement through your neighbor's property to get to yours, the only way to access your property would be by trespassing. And most neighbors don't like that very much. Some will even bring out their firearms to persuade you to quickly exit their property.

Some land has what is known as an **easement**. An easement is basically the grant or permission given by a landowner to use a portion of their property to access your property. If your property appears to be landlocked, you'll want to know if there is an easement on record with the county and you'll want to make sure that the neighbor property owners know about that same easement. You'll also want to know how wide the easement is and who has permission to use it. If there is no easement, you may have a very tough, uphill battle to obtain access into your property. A **right of way** is a type of easement that provides permission to use a pathway or road on another person's property without giving away ownership of that pathway or road. **Sometimes, the county, state, or federal government owns the right of way. Public roads and even some private roads can be considered right of ways.**

Practical:

Even though you may have legal access, you may not have practical access. For "practical" access, you will want to know about the physical road that leads into your property. Is there a road at all? If so, what are the road conditions like? Can you drive to the property in a standard sedan, or will you need a high clearance 4WD vehicle or an army tank? Can you get a camper onto the property? If the road is not useable, what will the cost be to make the access useable?

Many people looking to buy vacant land are looking to have a place of their own with no extra HOA or POA fees (for more on these, see the PRICE section below). But one thing to be aware of as it relates to the practical access is that an HOA or POA can be a good thing. Here's why. Say for example that you own a beautiful mountain property that is accessible by a 4-mile dirt road. But in the winter, it snows which means that in the spring that snow is going to melt and create washes and ruts in the road – especially when others drive on it when it's muddy and slick.

I owned a couple of mountain properties just like this not too long ago. They were simply amazing properties but unfortunately, there was no HOA or POA involved, and the roads stayed in terrible shape because no one wanted to pay the big money to hire a dozer operator to come in and grade the roads. As a result, the roads got worse and worse over time. Some properties will have a "road maintenance agreement" tied to ownership and if so, just know that most of the time, this is a really good thing as long as the annual dues are actually used to take care of the roads. Having everyone chip in a few hundred dollars each year to ensure good access and less wear and tear on your vehicle is much better than getting stuck in the mud or damaging your vehicle every time you want to visit your land.

THE 5-POINT
LAND BUYING
CHECKLIST

LOCATION
(20 Points)

Over the years, we've all probably heard someone say that the most important aspect of real estate is "location, location, location." While this may be true, please remember that a property located in the "best location" without access is still a property that has a serious problem.

But beyond this, location is incredibly important, so you'll want to find a location that meets your own personal objectives. As a silly example, a 5-acre lot on the beach of Kauai may be an amazing location but if you're wanting to hunt elk on your own land, you're going to go hungry. That's not going to be a good hunting property for you.

So, the value of the location is dependent upon what your purpose is for your land. Looking for a camping spot? Then a half-acre lot in New York City is a terrible location. Want a piece of land to build your restaurant on? A 2,000-acre ranch out in the middle of Wyoming may not be the best place to attract a lot of customers. However, the ranch sounds really nice to me!

Here are some things to consider as it relates to location:

Path of growth:

Many towns expand over time. Your job is to figure out which way the town is expanding. Is it expanding to the south? Then buying something 5-10 miles further south may prove to be the best long-term investment. Are there two growing towns 50 miles apart but nothing much going on in between them? Buying something right in the middle of both may be a great idea. To find out where the growth is headed, make a call into your local county building & permits department and ask where most of the new building permits are being issued for. Call the economic development office for the county and ask them what they see coming up in the months and years ahead.

Amenities:

What's around the land? Is there absolutely nothing for 100 miles? This could be a good thing if you're looking to build an off-grid getaway with privacy. At the same time, it may be a bad piece of land to buy if you're hoping to sell it to a developer. What shopping and grocery stores are close by? Are there medical service providers close by? What about the school systems?

Privacy:

When most people think about privacy, they think about no one around for miles. But it's amazing how much privacy you can still feel in the middle of a busy city but with trees and shrubs surrounding your land. But for the most part, people prefer at least some privacy. Is this property going to provide the privacy you'll be comfortable with?

Your Personal Interests:

As I touched on earlier, if you're looking for a hunting property, you'll really want to have a good understanding if the animals you want to hunt are anywhere around. Just because you buy 500 acres in Colorado does not mean that you're going to have elk on your property. Fortunately, you can download onX Hunt, a navigation app built for hunters. The app can help you understand what types of habitat exist on your property, and what species those habitats might attract. The key to this is asking yourself the question, "What do I personally enjoy doing and what else can I do on or around this property?

Local Attractions:

Are there national or state parks close by? Is there a substantial amount of public land close by? What lakes or rivers are around? Are there theme parks? Historical landmarks? Famous attractions? Generally speaking, the closer you are to these types of places, the higher the value your land will have and retain over the years.

Views:

Here's the deal: Everyone appreciates a nice view. I don't know of anyone in their right mind that is begging and screaming for a view of a junkyard. So, how would you rate the views of the land you're thinking about buying? Are you excited about them? Are they acceptable? Can they be improved with some tree clearing? You really want to make sure that you're comfortable with what you see from your land. Note: views usually don't improve over time; they typically get worse as others develop the surrounding area.

Neighbors:

I can't move on until we talk about neighbors. Neighbors can be the best or the worst. Years ago, I bought an absolutely beautiful property with some amazing views of the mountains. I wanted to put a small cabin on the place, but the southwest corner was about the only place I could put it without spending thousands and thousands more in tree clearing. So, that's where I put my cabin. I remember sitting on the front porch of my cabin and just thinking, *"This is the life! What an amazing property that I get to enjoy! What amazing views I have!"* And within a month of finishing it, the neighbor proceeded to put up a yurt only 50 yards in front of my cabin - right in front of my mountain views! In a very short time, not only were my views gone but my privacy went out the window. What happened next was nothing short of an episode straight out of *Sanford and Son*. They proceeded to turn my beautiful views into a complete junk yard. I wasn't happy at all but there was nothing I could do except sell my property before things got even worse. So that's what I did. So, what's the point? It's a good idea to get to know the neighbors **before** buying the property. Get a feel of who they are and what they intend to do with their own property before spending your hard-earned money. Of course, things can always change for the better or worse, but it never hurts to at least check on this before you buy. You'll thank me later!

THE 5-POINT
LAND BUYING
CHECKLIST

LAYOUT
(20 Points)

What if I told you I had 5,000 acres I'd sell you for just $10,000? As great as that sounds, there's a chance that it could be a terrible purchase. Here's why: what if that 5,000 acres was only 3 feet wide from beginning to end and the building setback requirements prevented you from building anything on it? Well, you've just potentially poured $10,000 down the toilet. I realize that such a property may not exist, but some properties are so narrow that about the only use would be for you to install an airstrip.

Typically, a great land layout would be something in the shape of a square or a rectangle. The further you go east, the **less** you'll see this (with curvy property lines) but the further you go west, the **more** you'll see this (with more straight lines). Seems like people got smarter during our westward expansion!

Having a layout with straight lines makes things easier on you in the long run. It cost less to fence in straight lines, it's easier to survey, setback requirements are much easier to figure out, and if you're like me, you just like things to be in a nice straight line anyway. It just looks better. With all this being said, I've owned multiple pieces of land with curvy and crooked lines. It's not always a bad thing but you just have to know your purpose in buying the land and if the layout will help you or hurt you in accomplishing your goals for the property.

Setbacks are also important when considering the layout of a property. For example, if a property is only 55 feet wide and the county has a required 30-foot setback for all buildings and improvements, you've got yourself a property you may not be able to build on. Check your plat map and other survey documents to understand what your setbacks are.

THE 5-POINT
LAND BUYING
CHECKLIST

DEVELOPMENT POTENTIAL
(20 Points)

As with the other items in this checklist, the idea of development potential is all subject to your purpose for the land. So again, know your purpose for buying and consider each of these items in your scoring.

Electricity:

Is there power available? If so, how close is it and how much will it cost you to bring it in? Who is the electricity provider for this area? Give them a call before you buy and ask what costs are involved. What is the cost for them to bring power in from the nearest pole or transformer? What is the cost to install a power meter? What is the cost to hook the power up to your house?

If power is not available, don't freak out. Solar power is becoming so much more common as well as affordable. For my own little mountain cabin, I bought and installed all my basic solar power system for just under $3,000.

Water:

Is there a water line available? If so, how close is it and how much will it cost you to bring it in? Who is the water provider for this area? What is the cost to run the line to your property? What is the cost to install a water meter? What is the cost to hook the water up to your home? Give them a call before you buy and ask them. If water is not available, don't freak out. Many people have drilled a well to meet the need. A quick note about wells though: A well can be an amazing convenience but just know that your driller is going to charge you just to set foot onto your property. Beyond that, he's going to charge you again for every single foot he drills down and there will never be a guarantee that he'll even hit water. Depending on the area, the driller may hit water at 10 feet, but he may not hit water until 900 feet or perhaps never at all. If you're thinking, *"That's a big gamble!"*, then you're correct. So, before deciding to drill, talk to your county building department or water resource office and ask if other wells have been successfully dug in the same area. If there is no water line around and if the gamble of drilling a well scares you, you have at least one more (and most likely more affordable) option. Install a water cistern. This is basically a large storage tank that you can fill with water you haul in or water from a rain catch system. Before installing a water catch system, make sure to contact your local county offices to see if this is even allowed. Some parts of the country will fine you for this.

Sewer:

Is there a sewer line available? If so, how close is it and how much will it cost you to bring it in and hook it up to your home? Who is the waste company for this area? Give them a call before you buy and ask what costs are involved. If sewer is not available, again, don't freak out. Many people have installed a septic system to meet the need. Septic systems are more common than solar power and water cisterns.

If you're going to install a septic system, make sure to do the following beforehand:

- Ensure that the county, HOA/POA, and any other governing authority affecting your land will allow it.
- Determine how big of a septic system you'll need. A septic system for a camper will be much more affordable than one for a 10,000

square foot home.
- Get estimates from licensed and insured septic installers. Unless you are experienced and trained, I would highly suggest you letting the professionals do this.
- Call references and check reviews for whoever you're thinking about doing the install.
- Get a perk test to ensure that your soil will work for a septic system. Some types of soil will just not work well.

Contour:

What is the slope of the land like? Flat land is easy to build on. Hills and mountainous properties can be built on, but the price increases due to all the dirt work, foundation work, and structural work that will need to be completed. Site prep can be one of the most expensive items in a building project.

Soil:

As mentioned in the septic system section, soil is a big deal. But just because the soil "perks" doesn't mean it's a great property to build on. Some soil may perk but it may be what is called "expansive" soil which means that it moves and would be terrible to build on. If you're planning to build, at the minimum, at least check to see if other homes nearby are being successfully built. You can even ask the neighbors for their insight and what types of foundation works best for building in the area. Make sure to ask a neighbor who's been living in their home in that area for at least a few years.

Flood zones:

This can be a big deal and can cost you tons of money if you're not careful. If you buy a piece of land in the hopes of building your dream home on it and later find out that the property is in a flood zone, it's going to mean one of two things is going to be true:

1. You're not going to be able to build at all or
2. It's going to add thousands and thousands of extra dollars to build in a way that the county will require in order for you to avoid water damage to your home.

So, check with your county building departments or FEMA flood maps to avoid buying land that won't allow you to build. On the other hand, you can also get a great deal on properties in flood zones. If all you're looking for is a place to camp on, ride ATV's on, or something like that, you can buy land in a flood zone for as much as 30-70% less than land that's not in a flood zone.

Zoning and Restrictions:

Zoning is an item that many overlook. Zoning refers to the intended usage assigned to a property by the county. Some common examples include agricultural, residential, recreational, commercial/industrial, and special district. Each county will have its own designated terminology and it's important that you understand what is allowed and what is not allowed in each zoning. Sometimes, land can be "re-zoned" but not without working with the county for approval and paying whatever fees are associated with the change. Also important to this discussion are **deed restrictions**. Deed restrictions are specific restrictions that are tied to the deed of the property. As an example, years ago, I was about to buy a beautiful mountain property in one of the most amazing locations in western Colorado. Everything was lined up until I saw the deed restrictions. The owner of the property also owned a large ranch across the road, and he insisted that certain deed restrictions were tied to the property I was buying so that his property would not be devalued. I could certainly understand this, but the list of deed restrictions was close to 5 pages long and had some restrictions that I wasn't really happy with. So, I backed out of the deal and moved on.

Bummer!

While we're still on zoning, it's important to talk about vacation rentals. Over the last 10-15 years, vacation rental properties have become more and more popular. If you're looking to buy land and build a vacation rental on it, just know that even though the property may be zoned for residential uses, the county may not allow you to run your vacation rental because they may consider that commercial usage. Make sure to check with your county zoning department to know what you can and cannot do. Also, just because the county zoning allows for this doesn't mean that your HOA or POA does. Check with them too! And one final note: thousands of people buy land every year in hopes of having a place to just go camping on. It's your land. So, you can camp on it right? Not necessarily. Some counties will not allow camping on vacant land and if they do, there are restrictions on how long you can camp, if tents are allowed, and if septic systems are required for medium to extended stays. Again, check with your county to know what you can do and what you can't do **before** buying your land.

THE 5-POINT LAND BUYING CHECKLIST

PRICE
(20 Points)

Notice that I'm putting price last on this list. Usually, when potential buyers look for land, price is the first thing they consider. But in reality, I think it should be one of the last things to consider. Just because a property fits your **budget** does not mean that it fits your **purpose**. Years ago, when we were looking to buy a home, our real estate agent said something I'll never forget. He told us to "*Buy a good home at a fair price.*" On the surface, that sounded really elementary to me, but as I've bought and sold real estate over the years, I'm coming to realize the value of what he said. Sometimes, it's more important to buy a property that you're happy with – even if you have to pay a little more than you'd like. Maybe you're not getting a discount or maybe you're just buying the land **at** market value. But if it's a property you're really happy with, then buying it will be a much better decision than getting a big discount on a property that you dislike. Buy a good property at a fair price.

Buying a good property at or below market value will nearly always be a good decision. Why? Because a good property usually **remains** a good property and increases in value over time. Newton's first law of motion which states that *"objects in motion stay in motion unless acted upon by an outside force"* generally applies to real estate as well. A good property usually stays a good property unless some outside circumstance changes it (such as a junky neighbor moving in, a liquor store building their store right next to the lot you bought for your dream home, etc.).

One final note on price. Remember that just as

you would have additional costs after buying a home (maintenance, upkeep, etc.), there are also some additional costs associated with buying vacant land. As a general rule, owning land is much less expensive to maintain than a house but there are still some costs that you should figure into your "real" price. Some of these costs include:

- HOA (Homeowner's Association) and/or POA (Property Owner's Association) dues
- Road maintenance agreement dues
- Property insurance
- Property taxes
- Drainage management (culverts, etc.)
- Dirt and site work
- Damage from weather (blown down trees, etc.)
- Loan payments and interest

THE 5-POINT LAND BUYING CHECKLIST

DUE DILIGENCE

Before we finish, I'd like to share a quick word about **due diligence**. What is due diligence? It is basically the inspection and research into the items associated with the purchase of your land that aren't so obvious.

The purpose of this e-book is to provide you with the **basics** of what to look for. It is not intended to be a comprehensive guide for every single aspect of buying land. The information here will be extremely helpful in getting you started but there are some due diligence items that are in addition to this checklist that can be even more important when making your land purchase. Because I'm not covering every detail here, please know that it's important that you complete your research on the property before you sign the dotted line. You will really want to have a good understanding of items related to the property you're planning to buy. Here are some due diligence items that are extremely important but not the scope of this e-book:

- Back taxes
- Liens (tax liens, mechanics liens, etc.)
- Encumbrances
- Judgements
- Title status
- Other items that may be "tied" to the property

A good land dealer, real estate agent, or title company can help you get started with this research so make sure not to leave this step out. You'll thank me later!

So, this is your **5-Point Land Buying Checklist**. I hope that this resource has helped you in your land buying adventure. Buying land can be extremely fun and rewarding but it can also turn into a nightmare really fast. As I've mentioned from the beginning, know your purpose, and make sure that the land you're buying will accommodate that purpose. The next best thing you can do is to find an experienced land dealer, agent, or broker who can help you identify the right property for you and your purpose.

THE 5-POINT LAND BUYING CHECKLIST

WE'RE HERE TO HELP

If you're looking for someone to help you in your land search, we would be honored to help you. At ZeteoLand.com, we are a Christian owned and operated land business whose mission is to provide you with the highest level of integrity, excellence, and simplicity in the land business. We have the experience, expertise, and proven track record to assist you with your next land investment. To provide you with the easiest purchase options, we sell land in two basic ways:

1. **Cash purchases:** We sell our properties at a discount ***below*** market value – anywhere from 5-25% below market value.
2. **Owner financing:** We provide owner financing on all our properties ***at*** market value but with an incredible 0% interest loan, no prepayment penalties, no credit

checks, and no loan applications. Everyone qualifies! Try finding this kind of deal at a bank. You won't!

If we can be of any service to you, feel free to contact us at the information below and we'll do our very best to help you.
Thank you so much for your time and interest!

Bryan Lark

Owner, ZeteoLand.com

info@zeteoland.com

(970) 765-8622

THE 5-POINT
LAND BUYING
CHECKLIST

SPECIAL BONUS OFFER: 10% OFF

As my gift to you for reading this e-book, I'd like to offer you a special 10% discount on any piece of land we have (not to be combined with any other sale or offer and special rules may apply). Just make sure to mention the discount code "**5POINT10**" and we'll be happy to apply this 10% discount for you. To receive this discount:

1. Visit ZeteoLand.com/featuredproperties and locate the property you want.
2. Email us at info@zeteoland.com with that specific property and the discount code above.
3. We'll be happy to apply your discount and get your land purchase all set up for you!

We look forward to serving you in your land search adventure!

Bryan Lark

Owner, ZeteoLand.com

info@zeteoland.com

(970) 765-8622

Integrity, excellence, and simplicity in the land business

www.ingramcontent.com/pod-product-compliance
Lightning Source LLC
Chambersburg PA
CBHW051534240526
45471CB00020B/2673